Learning Centre Ashton 6th Form College
Darnton Road, Ashton-under-Lyne OL6 9RL
Tel: 0161 330 2330

Return on or before the last date stamped below.

OFF THE WALL

ASFC LEARNING CENTRE

BLOOMSBURY

OFF THE WALL

FASHION FROM THE GERMAN DEMOCRATIC REPUBLIC

BLOOMSBURY

First published in Great Britain 2005

Copyright © 2005 by Here+There World Ltd
All photographs © 2005 akg images, London and Berlin,
and the photographers
The moral right of the author has been asserted

Bloomsbury Publishing Plc,
36 Soho Square, London W1D 3QY

A CIP catalogue record for this book is available from the British Library

ISBN 0 7475 8114 2
ISBN-13 9780747581147

10 9 8 7 6 5 4 3 2 1

Produced by Here+There
Design and Art Direction: Caz Hildebrand
Picture Editor: Lily Richards

Printed in China by Imago

All papers used by Bloomsbury Publishing are natural, recyclable
products made from wood grown in well-managed forests. The
manufacturing processes conform to the environmental regulations of
the country of origin.

www.bloomsbury.com

Introduction

East Germany may be most remembered for the activities of the Stasi, but now, for the first time, its secret flirtation with fashion is exposed.

Despairing of the drab, colourless apparel surrounding them, photographer Gunter Rubitzsh hired local models, chose the locations that inspired him — oil factories, worker canteens, concrete office blocks — and set about creating his own unique and daring style.

OFF THE WALL brings some of the Deutsche Demokratische Republik's most exotic fashion imagery to light. From blindingly bright mod go-go girls to demure country peasants posed with that most German of animals, the llama, these images run counter to everything we imagined went on behind the Berlin Wall. Was it intended as propaganda? A move to counter bourgeois Western values? Aspirational worker wear? We'll never know. What is certain is that what was produced in earnest is now a catalogue of camp.

Until recently, these fabulous spring/summer and autumn/winter collections have been hidden from Western eyes; but now, finally unearthed and collected together in this unique book, these glorious icons of a lost world are truly celebrated.

POLYESTER